MR. KEY'S SONG

ANOTHER REALLY TRULY STORY BY
SADYEBETH AND ANSON LOWITZ

GROSSET & DUNLAP · PUBLISHERS · NEW YORK

TO ALLURA
WHO ALWAYS SINGS
FOR HER SUPPER

Years and years ago,

when your grandfather's grandfather was a little boy, our country and England were fighting a war. The United States had once belonged to England and the English King just couldn't seem to remember that it didn't any more.

English sailors stopped American boats, way out on the ocean. They helped themselves to anything they wanted. They even took our sailors.

English soldiers made friends with American Indians and gave them guns and swords. The Indians put war paint on their faces and did war dances. This caused a lot of trouble. The Americans told the English they simply had to stop. The English said they wouldn't. Instead, they sent boats full of soldiers and sailors with cannons and guns to do all the damage they could.

First they went to Washington.

Now Washington was a brand new city with many nice new buildings. Our country's Capitol was there.

Without a bit of warning, the English marched into town. Everyone, even the President, had to move out in a hurry. Then the soldiers burned the White House. They burned the Capitol. They burned lots of the nice new buildings right down to the ground.

That done, they stole away like sly old foxes as fast as ever they could. They wanted to get back to their boats before the American soldiers could catch them.

However, they had not gone far when a terrible storm came up.
The sky was black as ink. In fact, it was so very dark that some
of the soldiers got lost and were left behind.

When the storm was over, they wandered into the garden of good old
Dr. Beanes. Here they sang and danced. They laughed and
shouted. In all, they were much too noisy.

The doctor was in need of sleep. He'd had a busy day. Calling down from his window, he asked them please to stop. But they were not at all polite to him and made twice as much noise as before.

After the doctor had stood it as long as he could, he had the
soldiers taken to jail. The jail was old and not very strong.
One of the men got away.

While he was on his way back to the English boats, he made up a
story about how mean Dr. Beanes had been to him.

So, when he told it to the Admiral, he didn't say one word about how mean he had been to Dr. Beanes. The Admiral believed the story. He was very angry indeed. He sent soldiers to find Dr. Beanes and bring him back at once. They came so very early that the doctor wasn't up. Without even giving him a chance to get dressed, they put him on a mule and made him ride in his night shirt through the woods to the shore.

Once on board the Admiral's boat, he was placed in chains and locked in the hold to wait till there was time to punish him.

Poor Dr. Beanes was very sad. Yet, he knew his friends would help him if they could. Everyone for miles around loved the grand old doctor. Whenever they were hurt or ill, they always sent for him to make them well again.

News of his arrest spread very fast. In no time, all his friends were talking about it. Something had to be done right away!

They thought and thought!!!

At last, one of his friends had a bright idea. He would ask Francis Scott Key to visit the English Admiral and tell him exactly what had happened. Perhaps, when the Admiral heard the truth, he would set the doctor free.

Francis Scott Key knew how to talk, making speeches was his business. He could make most anybody listen. Maybe the Admiral would listen, too. When Mr. Key was asked to go, he said he'd be delighted. He was always glad to help his friends.

Of course, boarding an enemy warship was a dangerous thing to do. The English might not let him come near, or, after he got there, they might decide to make him stay. However, Mr. Key was terribly brave. He said he'd leave at once.

First, he had to ask the President of the United States if it would be
all right. The President said, "Yes."

When everything was ready, Colonel Skinner decided to go along.
This pleased Mr. Key beyond words. The Colonel was as brave
as he was wise. He'd surely come in handy.

The two men sailed away in a tiny boat to find the English ships. They were some place near Washington, but just where, no one knew. After two whole days, they finally found them not far from Fort McHenry. Coming just as near as they dared, they waved a big white flag to let the English know they wanted to be friendly. The English Admiral waved right back for them to come on over.

The Admiral was most polite and listened with care to all Mr. Key
had to say. Then shaking his head, he told Mr. Key he did not
believe his story. The doctor simply had to be punished.

Mr. Key talked and talked. He coaxed and coaxed. He begged and begged. In fact, his speeches got so long, he used up nearly all the words he knew. Still the Admiral would not change his mind.

Just then, Colonel Skinner remembered that he had a pocketful of
letters from captured English soldiers. They wrote to tell the
Admiral how kind Dr. Beanes had been to them one time when
they were sick.

The Admiral was surprised. He could scarcely believe his eyes.

Yet, so pleased was he that he gladly went below to unfasten the
doctor's chains himself. He shook the doctor's hand and asked
to be forgiven.

The doctor was perfectly willing to forget the entire affair. So, he
said "Goodbye" to the Admiral for he thought he'd better be going.

Alas! Alack!!

The Admiral said he was frightfully sorry, but he was about to start
a battle. He was afraid that if he let the three men go, they
might tell the Americans what was going to happen.

Since he wanted to surprise them, this would never do. The doctor, the Colonel, and Mr. Key would have to stay until it was over. Excusing himself, the Admiral hurried here and there shouting orders to the sailors. Up came the anchors!

Away sailed the ships, straight for Fort McHenry! Closer and closer they came!! Soon they were so near, everyone could see the American flag waving above the fort. Then the battle started!!

The cannons boomed and zoomed! The rockets glared and flared!
BING!!   BANG!!!   BOOM!!!!
All day and all night the battle lasted. Hour after hour Mr. Key
  walked up and down the deck. He couldn't sleep a wink.

He was terribly worried. If the English kept on shooting that way, by morning the fort would be knocked into a million pieces. At last the night came to an end. Slowly the clouds of fog and smoke cleared away.

There, high above the fort, the American flag was still waving in
the breeze. Of course, it wasn't quite as good as new since one
of the stars had been shot away, but it looked better than ever to
the three men. They danced and shouted for joy.

Mr. Key, who could make up verses as well as speeches, quickly took an old envelope from his pocket and on it wrote the words for a song. It told how happy he was when he saw that the flag was still there when the battle was over.

When the English Admiral saw that no matter how hard he tried he couldn't knock the fort down, he decided to go somewhere else. Before he left, he let the three Americans go back to the shore.

As soon as Mr. Key got back to town, he showed his song to a friend. He liked it so much he rushed away to have it printed.

That night the song was sung in a theatre. The people cheered and cheered. Within two weeks everyone in the land was singing the beautiful song.

Although the song was written over a hundred years ago, we still
sing it just as it was written by Francis Scott Key on that famous
day. For now, it is our country's song, our own

STAR-SPANGLED BANNER

Oh, say, can you see, by the dawn's early light,
What so proudly we hailed at the twilight's last gleaming?
Whose broad stripes and bright stars, thro the perilous fight
O'er the ramparts we watch'd were so gallantly streaming.
And the rockets' red glare, bombs bursting in air,
Gave proof thro the night that our flag was still there.
Oh, say, does that star-spangled banner yet wave
O'er the land of the free and the home of the brave?

On the shore dimly seen thro the mists of the deep,
Where the foe's haughty host in dread silence reposes,
What is that which the breeze, o'er the towering steep,
As it fitfully blows, half conceals, half discloses?
Now it catches the gleam of the morning's first beam,
In full glory reflected, now shines on the stream:
'Tis the star-spangled banner: Oh, long may it wave
O'er the land of the free and the home of the brave.

And where is that band who so vauntingly swore
That the havoc of war and the battle's confusion
A home and a country should leave us no more?
Their blood has wash'd out their foul footsteps' pollution;
No refuge could save the hireling and slave
From the terror of flight or the gloom of the grave:
And the star-spangled banner in triumph doth wave
O'er the land of the free and the home of the brave.

O thus be it ever when freemen shall stand
Between their loved home and wild war's desolation;
Blest with vict'ry and peace, may the heav'n-rescued land
Praise the pow'r that hath made and preserved us a nation!
Then conquer we must, when our cause it is just,
And this be our motto: "In God is our trust!"
And the star-spangled banner in triumph shall wave
O'er the land of the free and the home of the brave!

CPSIA information can be obtained at www.ICGtesting.com
Printed in the USA
LVOW022140050112

262651LV00001B/30/P

9 781258 208448